PSALMS
OF
UNKNOWING

POEMS

HEATHER
LANIER

Monkfish Book Publishing Company
Rhinebeck, New York

Paperback ISBN 978-1-958972-06-9
eBook ISBN 978-1-958972-07-6

Library of Congress Cataloging-in-Publication Data

Names: Lanier, Heather Kirn, author.
Title: Psalms of unknowing : poems / Heather Lanier.
Description: Rhinebeck, New York : Monkfish Book Publishing Company, [2023]
Identifiers: LCCN 2023007050 (print) | LCCN 2023007051 (ebook) | ISBN
    9781958972069 (Paperback) | ISBN 9781958972076 (eBook)
Subjects: LCGFT: Poetry.
Classification: LCC PS3612.A5854 P73 2023 (print) | LCC PS3612.A5854
    (ebook) | DDC 811/.6--dc23/eng/20230308
LC record available at https://lccn.loc.gov/2023007050
LC ebook record available at https://lccn.loc.gov/2023007051

Book and cover design by Colin Rolfe
Cover art: "Hope II" (1907-1908) by Gustav Klimt

Monkfish Book Publishing Company
22 East Market Street, Suite 304
Rhinebeck, New York 12572
(845) 876-4861
monkfishpublishing.com

CONTENTS

III.
AND THE HOLY UNKNOWING...

IV.
AMEN

PSALMS OF UNKNOWING

Pumping Milk

Topless at the office
like a scandal,
I stand otherwise constructed—
trousers, polished black shoes,
hair a neat crop, the reds
of my face muted by beige smear.
My affair here is with
a machine. I'll soon hook up
with plastic trumpets, turn on
my motor, get milked
for a baby forty minutes away.
But it's this bare moment before
that stuns me, dangling braless
like half of me is made
for spring break gone primal,
the other half
will write a memo.
Is this what it means
to be a mother? The self, split
in two, like the body in labor?
Or is this just the tear
in humanity, even as we
shoulder-pad our denial—
always tugging us back
to the garden, to the beginning,
which wears the same
clothing as the end?

[I]

IN THE NAME OF THE MOTHER...

"Free Bible in Your Own Language"

Call me doubting Tom, but have you heard
my language? How I pepper the day
with *oh shits* of running late and roadkill?

And does a book on your table filter fables
through nineteen-eighties pop lines? *Shout, shout,*
let it all out? What about *shunyata*,

that wide bell of a Buddhist word—*emptiness*—
splattered flat on a blank page like a smacked fly?
In my bible, several vacant pages follow.

Let's shut one. Then, like a musical greeting card,
open it again. Any monks chanting
muddled nirvana? How about a bongo and a flute,

a woman at the top of a redwood rapping
the number of steps it took her to reach *now*?
Only text—Adam's rib and how Eve

was turned from it. This is wrong.
In my language, God takes two of his own,
blows bone-dust across a field

like seeds, plants trees. Roots grow into legs.
Upon what, you ask, is the book
written? Give me some space,

a quiet walk in the grass, unburdened
by your kiosk of Korean, Finnish, French....
With my footprints bending the blades,

I'll write a psalm of unknowing,
knowing the sun will erase it, will call it back
into straight, green, speechless strands.

Father Jim Shows Me Twelve Jesuses

in cinematic snippets, ten-second scenes of twelve Sons
          of man and, small eyes wide, he wants to know

which face, which frame, which meekest little finger
          captures the divine like aurora borealis

in a mason jar? The one kneeling in gravel, beard scruffy
          as a record store hipster, hands flailing a whirlwind

of precepts like he's conjuring religion from air?
          New shot, new film: meet the close-up Jesus

whose adages and all their archaeology blink gone
          the second you spot them: blue eyes

like small see-through planets, crystalline as the topaz
          in glass-encased crowns. Or how about

a clown, equipped with honey 'fro, sporting
          Superman tee and suspenders? This Jesus jigs

to the top of a New York high-rise, then weeps
          at the right hand of twin towers. Charmed,

bored, bemused—I still don't see
          what I need, and what

do I need? A person of color? An androgynous mother?
          Even another—rectangular jaws made larger

by cropped hair and a rough goatee—is, at first,
          just another modern man

playing God, or trying to, and don't I see that
          childish need whenever the rearview reflects

my gritted teeth, my squint-eyes raging at a road that won't go fast
          enough for the dashboard's digital clock

that's also mine and always ticks for me?
          But then a dozen villagers in burlap robes

ask a bowl-cut Jesus *why*, and *what*, and *who*,
            and this one, this one gulps

at doubt, then airs it out
            by words of wide Bronx vowels

like his is a draft he's surprised by, like
            who knew he'd find metaphors of stone?

Like his father is weird as the eyes
            of a spider, like he's learning his religion as he goes.

Bed Rest

Cramps I say, and the midwife
says *Culture*, cranks

the metal beak. A fold in me cringes—*aw-easy*.
Then a swab, then a vial

thin as a cigarette
like she's about to smoke the cells of my cervix.

It's tricky business, growing three hundred bones,
a pair of eyes that haven't seen

tsunamis on TV or tulips in spring.
I watch both from the couch while reporters

count down to a government
shutdown like anxious new year's hosts

who think the ball will burst,
coat Manhattan in something toxic.

The nation's parks will close, the deer
absolved of deer-ness, the Veterans' names

unread on the walls,
the trees stoic in their underfunded bark.

We're waiting. We fear it,
the *uh-oh* of silence, so we watch the end

of days in theaters—
icebergs melting a map's coasts,

all green gone
gray. But look—buds on the trees,

grass waking in patches,
and the walls of the nursery painted fern green

for someone thirty weeks in the making
and already a heart beating

one hundred and forty blips a minute.
See? the midwife shows the digits

on the doppler. My baby—
she's either underfunded, shutting down,

or content, clueless to the tune
we wail out here: *What if,*

what if the worst? The worst
sometimes occurs. *Ten weeks,* the doctor

said over my father's body, his organs
dialing down as fast as this one's lit up.

Ode To Seven

*Everybody knows that there is a finite span of immediate memory
and that... this span is about seven items in length.*
— George A. Miller, *The Psychological Review*, 1956

List all the coincidences you can remember:
days in a week, pillars of wisdom, lucky dice, seven
deadly sins, original planets, seas, world wonders.
Mathematicians, seeking a perfectly random deck, fathered
the rule of seven card shuffles, also the number of times
Levitical priests sprinkled blood from the red heifer's body.

I know. I'm not the first to marvel at seven's body
of work. Jews and trivia experts might remember
that Jericho landed in Joshua's hands once he circled it seven times,
that God's first line, which begins *in the beginning*, is seven
Hebrew words, and bam: genesis. *Why did our Father
mark the world with this number?* Christians wonder.

And Pythagoreans, eating numbers instead of bread, wondering
about every digit, gave them gendered bodies,
called seven *perfect*. Same with numerology. Your father
might score Marilyn Monroe a *ten*, but if he remembered
how to turn names into numbers, he'd know she equals *seven*,
a perfect Pythagorean male. Seven can turn on us: the time

in years for the devil's contract to conclude, the number of times
you sign your name. Not just for wonders,
it means omens, evil—seven seals, seven plagues, seven
hells. Here's one that haunts me: our bodies
need seven years to regenerate their cells. I remember
this lesson from my doctor, my father.

It implied immortality in multiples of seven. My father's
body ended that math seven years ago. Those "times
tables" don't just add—they subtract. I can't remember
if his cologne was sandalwood or citrus. About his eyes, I wonder...
It doesn't matter. This year, he'd have a whole new body
anyway. Grief wails the first year, but by the seventh

it whispers. The quiet is maddening. Into prime seven's
slender leg on which, like a stiff crane, it stands, my father
slips. Into its wholeness, into the whole dark (and light) body
of the world which builds anew in seven days. How much time
does it take to lose all we have? The mind can wonder
all it wants, but the body stores memory, and new cells don't remember

what they never knew. Father, I'm sorry. I don't remember
the precise span of your arms around my body. In another seven
years' time, what other of your wonders will I lose?

The Messiah Could Have Gotten Listeria

"Eating for two?"

– *What to Expect When You're Expecting*

Mary, did they wag their fingers *no*
at unpasteurized milk? Did you have to count
your protein for too little and your tuna

for too much, fretting mercury might metalize
the haloed brain of the divine?
You had no sonic wand snooping the precise size

of the incarnate's kidneys,
no weight-gain *tsk tsks* or glucose tests.
You had, of course, the risk of infection.

How did you carry the earthquake
of history, like a big bang
contained in the squash-sized babe?

When you watched Joseph's tired gait ahead,
did you heed the warning:
your thoughts could do your child harm?

You could sing the wrong songs?
You could love the God you carried
incorrectly? You could fuck this up?

Mary, all I've got inside me is another human
and men still give up their seats,
women sing odes to my stomach,

and crazies blow up buildings
because they think the being in my belly
weighs the world. The doctor says

I weigh too much. How did you
handle the pressure, Mary, carrying
not the weight of the world

but the weight of its maker?
Did you place your hand on your belly,
take a breath, and trust

that this world, and all the things in it,
would not kill him?
That you were enough?

"Jesus Might Have Walked on Ice," Scientists Say

Spring ice—
as hard to see as miracles,

as Mother Mary
in a slice of burnt toast—

probably
didn't float on Galilee. Today

the sea goes by
Kinneret, and scientists measure

its freshwater
depths and temps in fine-point, blue-ink

graphs that climb
and dip like 2-D valleys *yay* their minds

walk through.
There's no chance, as Greenland melts,

that rising Kinneret
would freeze today anyway.

But this
is what they find for Jesus' time:

two days
of rare cold did befall them.

Salt springs
emptied into the pool, hit bottom,

rushed up
in plumes, and barely seen spring ice

might have formed.
Odds are slim. They say, at best *one time*

in thirty years,
perhaps *one time in sixty*. The science

can't state a single
thing sturdily, like *it is I, be not*

afraid,
as it strides on its impossibility.

Its burden
is one of actuality. *Might have, could have:*

words that crack
a claim like feet on frozen water.

What faith
it takes to go on even that.

Forecast in the Thirty-First Week

Think happy thoughts. Studies show your baby can sense your mood.

How will this rain wrong-do you?
Will my cursing the concrete sky
all spring infuse you with malaise,
the cheese between your future teeth
too trite, the wine not right?
I've tried, for your sake, to love
this state. The winter was so cold
every molecule clenched frost
in a fist. Forgive me.
Your sky is your ground
is your wall of red womb.
My heart is a whirling fan you live by—
it quickens at the ticker headlines.
Yesterday, three girls who'd graced
ten years of missing person posters
were found. Their captor claimed
they loved him, beat the babies
out of their bodies. I shouldn't tell
you this. The world is a place of pillows
and knives, both indifferent to us.
The world is a place of hands
that you, my dear, must learn to trust
and hands you must never go near.
Nine more weeks my chemistry
will eke into yours for, as sweaty
couples vow, *better or worse*, and I'll try
to ladle myself into loving
just about everything—the rain,
a strip of fast-food chains, a baby
the rapist let one victim bear—
so each cell you wake anew to
is sent the fortune smaller than
even paper slips in cookies:
all is well, all is well, all is well in this world.

"Bear Leads Police in Wild Chase

Through Streets of Anchorage,"
but yesterday a cop shot a man

who witnesses say was reading a book.
I only trust things that take a long time,

a friend said, *like books and trees.*
Two thousand five hundred feet

per second is how fast a bullet moves, a hundred
thousand times faster than a blink,

a decade faster than a book.
The cop believed the book was not

a book but a gun. In God's thesaurus,
is a book the opposite of a gun?

Last week another Black man had car trouble,
walked toward the siren with hands up.

Lives take nine months of nausea, I know,
each hour an eon as I stroke my belly,

try to keep food down. Lives take
years to be old enough to fear, although

less than eighteen, as many mothers know.
My babies come out slow and white.

A bullet is the opposite of a baby.
What book was he reading? The screen

doesn't say. Did our reader love chemistry?
The classics? His son? No word.

Instead, the website reports
that rioters in Charlotte smashed windows

and the bear jogged by a Pizza Hut
but no one was hurt, not even the bear.

My Form of Yelling

"This is my form of yelling."
–*Project Runway* finalist Edmond Newton,
watching his fashion show

My form of yelling is to swallow. The yell travels the body's length, implodes.

The gunman's form of yelling was to finger the trigger, then fire. Five times in a deserted parking lot.

The victim was once a baby. I held him after birth. Twenty years later, a cop held him in the lot as he looked up, up, up into the stars of Pittsburgh.

Let's call the victim *the boy*, although he grew older than boys.

Google will show you his mug shot. *See there, the boy's name tattooed on his neck. See there, his dilated eyes.*

Memory's form of yelling is to protest with blurred photographs: he, the bottle-fed baby. He, the bunny-eared toddler we loved. At age twelve I learned, *Hold the head like so.*

The cop didn't yell. He filed paperwork.

My mother's form of yelling is to plan the perfect funeral. The prayer cards might feature crowns.

The boy, did he yell? No one reported as much. A neighbor recounted five gunshots. The pathologist found three in his chest.

The news anchor doesn't yell. She flashes very white teeth and says crime has increased in Pittsburgh.

Yesterday we heard gravitational waves for the first time. One wave: an island-sized heart beating into a canyon. The other wave: the chirp of a bird in that canyon, echoing back.

The universe doesn't have to yell. The universe holds objects so massive they bend the fabric of the space-time continuum.

What happens to your love when it is bent into a headline?

If two people dance around each other, they'll cause ripples in space-time so miniscule no scientist can measure them.

I envy the fashion designer. I want to make dresses. I want to sew floor-length gowns from the fabric of space-time. I want to wear them and waltz the boy back to me.

There have been 219 days this year and 407 mass shootings. America's form of yelling is two turntables and a microphone-shaped gun.

My form of yelling is to kneel in a church and refuse to pray. The non-prayer tackles the air, no angels there. Only sunlit floating dust.

The gunman needs a muzzle. A yoga master. A head chopped off.

That's the ancient form of yelling—revenge. Creaky as a guillotine.

If he and I now danced around one another, could we still ripple the space-time continuum?

No. Ghosts have no mass. They are outside the years.

He emerged a little after midnight. He was blue, and loved, and love. He was asked, by way of a smack, to scream.

We all start there. A baby's form of yelling is to yell.

Rush Hour Commute, Good Friday

My child will have
two shoulder sockets.
Just a few fingers
wrapped around a wrist
and someone
could yank the bone-ball
from its cradle.
I grip the wheel,
check my speed—
seventy. Flesh
is too fickle, the body
too injury-prone
to house us for long.
Yesterday a friend,
mid-forties, died
on her way home.
Farmland passes,
and I amass the images:
face in the fractured
windshield, car turned
over and up
in smoke. Five
minutes ago, I sank
the speedometer's
needle down to zero
against a blur
of sudden brake lights,
and the tires of a mini van
behind me bloomed smoke.
In my rearview
the red beast
swerved onto the shoulder.
The hair of the driver
flew forward. When her head
fell back against the seat,
her eyes were wide

into the future
of her final breath,
averted today. Today
is Good Friday, and now
I veer right, merge
with the light
eastbound traffic.

Trauma-Informed Christ

How did His golden psyche not split
when they drove the first nail
between two metatarsals?
Did He not hunger
to be held when the thorn scraped
His holy skull?
You can't be fully human
without aching
for the divine kiss He contained.
What did it cost our God
to get cut? A friend took a blade
to his knees in parallel lines
because his mother used a wall
to drum his skull.
How did He not cower
from Man thereafter, flee
our perpetual cries for better jobs
or dates, swat away
our stupid requests for more?
His hands held proof—
flesh punctured never heals
the same. If you're both fully God
and fully human, Jesus,
how were you not half-
triggered by yourself?

The Making

Where my belly once rumbled
you roll, my hunger pangs
replaced by another's need for space.
Where a boy's hands would slip
through the inward dip to carve
a sexy shape from air,
my hourglass is blown full,
sands no longer sifting
through the small neck of seconds.
My body's packed, a bulbous
water-slow clock of waiting.
It is strange, my dear, the making:
I make you living, and you make
what we living rarely know—
nine months of never empty,
never alone.

Before Writing Back to a Friend Whose Mother Is Dying,

you stare at the empty fireplace.
Don't make it a metaphor.

That the soot in the fireplace has smothered
every brick but where the fire burned,
that the bricks now hold a ghost
of flames that once flickered there

doesn't mean anything.
Just write your friend back.

You have to figure out how to fill
an email with nothing
but a bed of silence, and the silence

can't be empty,
though it must be empty of your own grief.

Your grief is an ornery dog
that wants to play. Tell it to sit.
Then it will offer the obvious from its teeth like a bone:

Metaphors of sunsets will make you both barf.

Everything happens for a reason
is the greeting card from an unlikable god.

This too shall pass is precisely the problem,
the word *pass* like a swoosh, so fast
it's gone.

Tell her you'll lie down next to her. Tell her
whatever mad throb her heart drums out,
you'll let yours do the same.

Do not dare tell her the truth:
That it will be like screaming into a black hole,
the wanting

so bad her body will think it's grown
a thousand arms, grabbing what's gone.

That she might fall into the hole
and that no one,
        not even you, can join her.

The World Turns Too Fast

for a woman of two.
Racing fuel
the pump spews
beside regular
unleaded. I hold
my breath. Overnight
the petals bloomed.
Quakes crushed
the coast, some
famous face
will die soon, and
senators are set
to snap the lights
out on the nation's
news to prove
some point about
a woman's right
to not choose.
But here you are—
three pounds big,
a wanted
cabbage cornered
in the womb.
Just stay put.
Your eyes
can open, your
ears can hear
the horns the
heartbeat the hollow
in the bowl left
empty in a field.
Listen—the ticking
will always tock
its way to now
and now will long
for then. Tomorrow

comes screeching in.
I'll waddle you
out and in
twelve months
you'll toddle
toward some stray
jagged thing
from which I must
with all I am
keep you safe.

Your Heartbeat

used to be a flutter, a hummingbird's
blurry wing buzzing
a half-inch of spring.

Is the want, my barely baby,
as simple as that
single grass blade
being, in this new season
of green, its bendable self in the sun?

Now you're a runner
barefoot through a lush, wet forest.
Determined. Compelled

by what, I wonder?
Chasing nothing but another
and another and another
beat? The chance to be

in a new now—

[II]

AND THE CHILD...

Only a Sliver of Love Runs Hot

Only a sliver of love runs hot
like the movies: gallivanting in rain
with a lover, breaking to eat face
against a brick wall while the downpour
drenches your bob.
                          Only a chunk of love
cushions like cotton batting in baby-wash
commercials: flushed mother touches
her lips to the Q-tip toes of a newborn,
euphoric in her oxytocin swell.

Love too is the violent wail arcing
over your showerhead, yanking you—again—
to the baby's hunger. Shampoo foams
an eye-burning halo. Love is the wine-
red rage for the one you married
and the lit fleck of forgiveness
floating in a glass, faint as the fuzzy glow
of the closest galaxy. *Don't look straight at it,*
astronomers say, *or you won't see.*

And love is sometimes looking head-on,
kneeling on public bathroom tile, inches
from my daughter's crotch so I can clean
the crevices of shit. Because her hands
impersonate the wings of fluttering birds,
I might do this until one of us dies,
half numb at the altar of that amorphous
aching engine we pretend to squeeze
inside the shape of a valentine heart.

I wipe and keep getting brown,
like I've done since she was swaddled,
when passers-by pegged my entirety
in pink. *Squishy. Motherly. Soft.* They forget
this whole endeavor begins with blood.

To the Comic Who Says Her Critic Is Missing a Chromosome

The baby is down by ten tonight
and I've cracked your book's spine to laugh
myself out of my life: a calendar
of doctors for her heart, kidneys, brain,
eyes. My kin has been metonymized
for medicine.
                    Get this. Nine-eleven-
eleven was the day she first giggled,
eyes lit by a church's stained glass,
toothless gums exposed like Swedish fish
as the preacher alluded to but didn't name
what the news had played and re-
played that day.
                    Anger can try to fill
the hole, say grief counselors, a fact
my clenched jaw knows in too-fast runs.
But I return sweaty, and the hole
in my daughter's heart remains
and you write in your Emmy-Award-
winning way, *that asshole's so dumb
he must be missing a chromosome.*
How many genes does it take to change
a heart?
          Too soon? asked the comics
a year after, the skyline behind them
a scar of loss.
                    I shut your book and hear
a thump. My baby's arms helicopter-chop
the air. Her eyes are closed, her mouth
a devious grin. In waking she can't yet
lift her head. I poke my husband.
We peer over the bassinet,
giggling at the little ninja
whose fighting off what exactly?
How can she have enemies already?

Etymology of Apocalypse

It means not
          a dozen atom bombs
                    or a hazmat plague

or a ghost-ash earth
          without footprint.
                    It's not a noun

of weight, not an asteroid
          or a hammer. It's the grammar
                    of movement

across a room, around
          a planet: to uncover.
                    Reveal. Disclose.

Remove our steel
          armor, silk gowns.
                    Strip our lives

of that which conceals:
          gloss, grin, *good.*
                    Be done

dressing each day
          in yesterday's gold
                    medals. Face—all eight

billion of us—
          a mirror or a lover
                    or just the dark,

willing to rewrite
          daily the world
                    with our baring.

Things I Heard After My Baby Was Born

I can't imagine what you're going through.
It doesn't look like anything's wrong.
What I imagine is can't.
You're anything, going through wrong.

Did you take drugs while pregnant?
People with her syndrome are intellectually disabled.
Her syndrome drugs people.
You intellectually disabled pregnant.

She's not damaged goods.
You can always place her in a home.
She's a home.
You cannot always place her.

I'm sorry.
Special babies happen to special people.
Sorry, special babies.
Sorry, special people.

It's either she's bad seed or you're bad soil.
Nothing will change the fact that you love her.
Nothing will change the seed of the fact:
It's either bad or you love her.

Congratulations! You need to test her kidneys.
You'll always grieve the child you thought you'd have.
You need the child you have.
Congratulations, you'll grieve.

Fighting with My Husband Over Alphabet Puzzle Cards

Alas, each half makes a whole, like men joking
better half but never wives. *A* fits with *Apple*,

C with *Cat*, *M* with a blue-suited gent
dreaming of *W* for *Watermelon*. There is no woman. No child

either. Briefcase in hand, he totes faith in himself
forever, or whenever we toss these things.

God almighty, I think, hovering
hands-and-knees over the mess of cards, so

I stir an old war: Who does more, a knock-knock
joke with no punchline. We both work to

keel. A friend posed a question on-
line today: *What do you wear to feel empowered?*

Maxi dresses, women wrote. *Palazzo pants. Sturdy shoes.*
No men replied. We can

only imagine: having no need to capture
power like kids catch fireflies in July, grubby hands

quarantining glows. At last, one guy
relayed: *I can wear anything*.

Sweetheart, when I say *Don't call me Lady*, I mean
There is no card for my kind. I mean I love you but

underneath our lives are ten thousand years.
Vows join hands but trail ancient equations, men minus

women. I miss cupping fireflies, peering into the
exalting dome of my hand. That's what the girls did:

yielded to light. The boys I knew plucked them in two,
zagged bioluminescence across their foreheads.

Upon Learning that Our Baby Can Swallow Her Own Spit

Victory in the black branches that did not crack off
in the night, did not smash our four-door
or decapitate the cat.

Likewise, the sky
which miraculously held. The birds too
stayed mostly afloat

or slept. Crisis averted. Come spring
they'll carry—most of them—twigs
for nests, worms to drop inside beaks

so small they could pick a lock.
Victory is the millions of un-extinct species, this day
an added ho-hum page to turn

in the reference books of their Latin-named histories.
That's you,
red-bellied woodpecker, and you, Spanish lynx.

Congratulations to your non-demise!
Let us go on, all of us—
inhaling clouds

of molecules that haven't killed us,
not in this moment, not in the last,
eggs and sperm still sensing

toward becoming, so they can join the world's many
and the few
born with the incapacity to swallow.

Sperm

Don't let their tadpole shapes
fool you. They lack a heart,
a stomach, a set of eyes. They're luggage
and propulsion, a sack of genes
and the motor to deliver.
They hunt for their half-self,
some queen cupped
by the sponge-hands of biology,
all atoms around her
singing an A-note of *Aw*
to her rotund, planetary self.

When he comes, mouth open,
toes wiggling, he's caught
like a word in the throat
between a million pasts—
cavemen coaxing fire,
his shy bird-watching grandpa—
and a million futures.
What if the wrong one reaches?
The Marine Corps-worthy
obstacles are many—ten thousand
lengths of their bodies,
the Skee-ball score of the cervix,
two tubes *a la* Frost's
two roads and only one will do.

Earth is the perfect distance
from the perfect-sized star
due to what? *Luck*? Or that other,
chipper phrase, typed
in the chapter of the alternate book
I'm meant to read: *Happens
for a reason*? Please make it so:
that some grand hand
orchestrates each life

like a symphony we can't hear
as anything other than clanging
because we're too far or too close.

To the Parent Who Says Her Child's Disability Isn't in "the Natural Order of Things"

The Earth holds amoeba, oceans, grass, the pop tune
on everyone's repeat radio,
                              an argument with
a husband, my forehead in my hand after hearing
your remark.
                    People who chew and people
who cannot. People who see and people who cannot.
People who walk and people who do not.
                                        What's
the natural order? Nesting dolls, red dresses
splattered with gold blooms?
                              Can you fit your grief
into your purse into your love into your medical bills?

Or is the natural order a Darwinian poster? The human
ever upright in each outline?
                              Get taller, Mother.
                    Watch your ducks behind you
waddle taller, too. Keep them in a row.
                                        But we can't.
You and I shall outlive our children or leave
them in the care of others.
                              Our family albums
are fat with what some call *atypical,* but the weight
of them doesn't tremble the planet's orbit a lick.
Feeding tubes, seizures, diapers until when
                              we don't know.
                    What is the order of seconds in a memory?
Don't say chronology. Even the distance from one planet
to the next bends time.
                    It's true, your child won't care
for himself. Nor will mine.
                    Nor did the elder caveman
whose fossilized bones show he never chewed.

His friends did it for him. You wanna tell them
their compassion
                    broke the natural order?

Your Eyes, My Daughter, Are Genius Caliber

I spot the five-pointed star in your iris
like a chunk of the cartoon heavens
sought a long, enduring swim.
Your gloss-black pupils reflect
my stressed brow

easing into adoration. I see you
seeing me — mother struck
by the ancient wonder:
what impossible mathematics
in the molecules of your seeing.

A brain to move a hand to swipe my hair.
Ears to catch the peripheral
hey, and you turn to face
a face your mind already mapped — the giver
of food, love. And all your vowels

riper than fruit in the wooden bowl,
your oohs and ahs and ehs
whole as grapes in your mouth. They say
you don't meet your milestones.
That the arm of one chromosome

has a hiccup in its copies.
But you are living. You sense. You suck
your thumb. You receive
the world, your awareness a daily haiku.
This morning something caught

your eye a long infant-minute
and I thought you were zoning out
on window light, or worse, seizing.
I got down to your level
and saw it:

a windchime glimmering
against the suburban winter scene, the brass

tubes lit by a low sun. *See it*,
your staring said, that star
in your iris dazzled.

The Vigil I Don't Yet Explain to My Three-Year-Old Daughter

We held candles in a train
of mostly women

in the night   Gave silence a voice
to say   No,

not in the dark
The things done to the woman beside me

in the dark   How it
taped her mouth shut

The way a man used the dark to say   Tell no one
and it never came to light

was not unlike the man
on your U.S. Presidents handout

You color his face
Don't even have to ask   he said

You color him teal   *They let you*   he said
Make sure you ask   we mothers say

He said   on a tape   in the day
in the light   *They let you do it*

And it came to light   That's how the phrase goes
It came to light

No trial   no verdict
Just a hundred glowing faces in the night

Psalm For Doctor Normal

Bless the Doctor, O my soul
        and my daughter's soul
and all my daughter's missing genes
        shall bless His holy degree.

My daughter's shortness, bless Him
        for He blesses her with a laugh
through His nostrils when I show Him
        a photo of her with classmates.

Bless Him, her scoliosis
        for He sees it, and measures the curve
in degrees (forty) and seeks
        to straighten it or can't and leaves,

head shaking, in favor
        of other bodies to be made more right.
Bless Him, O my daughter's heart
        for He will hear it and tell me

the murmur's barely there
        like His finding nothing
took an evil something
        away. Touch His finger, O you

undiagnosed soul, for He will make you
        not a Michelangelo
but the body you knew not you were,
        the labeled body, the wrong body,

housing your being like a planet
        squeezed into a carport.
He is the perfect Doctor of dissection.
        He is the one true Doctor.

Do not worship false Doctors.
        Now lay my daughter's body
on the altar, and my body, too
        because I made her.

Bless the Doctor, O my body,
        which is bell-curved
which is aching, which is aging,
        which looks upward,

sees the knife blades, hears
        His baritone: *Take two*
of these and call me, no, don't
        call me I'll call you.

The Christian Ladies Talk Infertility

Tell the listeners your story, one says
to the other and the other
says they tried everything—herbs, acupuncture,

angels, in vitro. *I couldn't even speak
to God,* she says. *I couldn't hear
God through my anger.* We feel her

as they say—until the lab coats
or the petri dish or the Creator
gave her five embryos, and she sings

this bit with gospel-choir alleluia:
*They were healthy embryos. I mean,
these were good*

quality
embryos, and the airwaves don't offer enough static
to silence the podcast's tacit crash.

So much to celebrate, she sings, *so much
to praise the Lord for*
like when your God makes good

as consumer protection agent, like when
your Almighty delivers top-notch DNA
and the egg the doctor rejects doesn't even show

so there's no need to crucify it
before a crowd of athletes and critics
and mothers and strapping male twins.

Anger Choice Cards in My Daughter's Backpack

When I get angry I....
Take a brain break:
Two kids bend their bodies
into upside-down L's.

Breathe deeply:
A skinny lady sits cross-legged.
Behind her, a field of clouds.
Remember a happy time.

Remember when your world
was a top spinning at a party
for a kid whose name you
don't remember. Take your mind

elsewhere. *Walk away,*
reads the one with a boy's back
to me, holding cards
on how to shut down anger

about anger cards.
The world is on fire.
You are not permitted
to meet it with fire.

You are permitted
to fold your anger
like a kerchief, let it peek
from your pocket for color.

This is your anger, my husband says
and briefly burns
his eyes into mine:
a cage and the tiger inside it.

You can take to the streets,
the cards don't say.
You can shout
into the closed doors

of the neighbors. *Throw over*
a table, reads the card
even Jesus
carried in his linens.

Jesus Doodles

Jesus bent down and wrote with his finger on the ground.
—John 8:6

What's he etching in the sand?
After the men grab their rocks, aim
at the woman who wronged them
with her yes, or no not hollered
loud enough, he kneels to write
what? A psalm we've never heard?
An anthem for a country
we've never seen? Or why
words? Does God-
in-human-form like portraiture,
the bottom lip of his mother?
Maybe something more practical
from his omniscient well: a map
of the ocean floor. A topography
of forgiveness. A formula
for how to travel faster than light,
which they say we'll only live long enough to do
if we can keep ourselves
safe from ourselves, each other.
The bigger miracle was never
water to wine but our brute hearts
softening enough to pause
our pitching arms, drop the plot
to crush the other, like my damn
neighbor—khakis pressed,
arms crossed with rightness that rewind me
to a church basement
where balding men told women
get behind or become a woman stoned.
Their savior, so certain—
biceps blazing, ready to rip
the lock off a vault of treasure.

Mine—an asker of questions,
a squatter in sand, doodling hearts
and spirals small as minor sins.

Skipping Stones

Think of the way you cast that apple core
between the trees. Your dad derided, *girl throw!*
and you thought he meant, not hard enough.
You thought he meant, annihilate the seeds,
white meat, and stem with Popeye arms. Be male,
destroy, smash it at the trunk. But now,

You have to pivot from the waist, like this,
your husband shows you when you sink the stone
you want to skip. His hips torque like a dancer,
or a woman baiting *come-hither* with her hour-
glass shape. Just choose another bit, the flattest
limestone shard. No matter. Down it plunks.

You've got it wrong, still willing the rock
to skip by force, the way your father hacked
the hedges, opened jars, plowed snow, built walls
between his son and him. *Not mine*, he said,
not anymore, not since your brother hit
his own bride. Once in the jaw, twice in the eye.

Try again, your husband says. Whip your body
like a trebuchet. Turn it, snap the hip
and let your elbow follow, see? And there
his stone skims clear across the water
like a finger feeling glass, like your mother's hand
would wipe the kitchen table. *Therapy,*

she called it, rope-spine taut and curled above
a stain. Like prayer, like pleading, she gave over
every cell to cleaning floors. *You have to use
your whole body.* He rests his fingers at
your sides, pulls the left back, thrusts the right,
says *pop,* repeats the motion. *Feel that?*

You hear the *Pop* your brother cried before
your father's casket closed, the sobs your mother
wears in every bone, your brother's lone

apology, the time you told your husband,
fuck yourself. How masculine it felt,
so you threw a hammer too. And now

you feel your husband's ring against your side,
the swerve his body makes from behind, the way
he moves you from the core, the grace that follows
force, the reward. You feel the distance
to the other shore, his breath on the back
of your neck, the smooth stone, and you let go.

[III]

AND THE HOLY UNKNOWING...

My Family and I Disagree about Politics

We will always get naked for the surgeons.
Our bodies will be laid before them, dense as sandbags.

They will operate no matter who we named our leader.
They will remove gangrenous bits, slice out polyps.

Fathers will not even think to ask that they excise our next rally cry.
Mothers will not inquire if our opinions can be scooped out, too.

Our beloveds will bite nails as they wait, fall in love with our physicians,
however briefly. The stitches always disintegrate.

Skin finds itself again, like a split sea, although sometimes it takes staples.
Sometimes you have to puncture the body to hold it together.

Loving Thy Right-Wing Neighbor

It's accidental—our tiptoe toward
the political sinkholes
as we yawn at twilight on
your (literally) greener grass.
My quick chicken recipe
reminds you of long work hours
which jabs awake the shot
they want your arm to take.
I step away, remember you
might be even more contagious
than me. Venus is so far
the only wink in the sky.
We swat at our ankles, talk
mosquito spray, the FDA, *oops*—
and my mental crossing guard
emerges yellow-jacketed,
stop sign held straight out.
You were the first to knock
on our door, offer your number.
Next month your church will erect
foam tombstones for fetuses,
a Halloween trick turned sad.
Mine's got a sign that says people
who never step foot in yours
matter. I haven't been this tired
since pregnancy, I say and you
agree. If we talk of summer heat
in fall, we'll skirt the edges
of the cause. It's not our fault
our nation's alleluia
is an ode to what's left over
after bombs. Here's something
I might say in tomorrow's
unseasonable weather:
Did you know a church
beside the towers stayed

upright, unscathed? Not a single
broken pane. The sycamore
that blocked it from the blast
is now a stump. On break
from recovering bodies,
the first responders slept
in pews. Their jackets—
the same caution yellow
as my inner crossing guard—
became pillows beneath
their sooty faces.
Alarm had folded
for once into what
it never gives us: rest.

The War We Barely Knew

It brought no brass horns
to brandish a blaring, shiny A-note,
no hand-beat sheepskin drum to keep

the time. We only heard
the steady rush-hour wind of cars
down our residential road

and all that came for us was the fog rolling off the bay
like a blanket of white batting
unfurling up the roof-clad hill

in record speed, overtaking peaks
of evergreens, scalloped roof tiles and phone wires.
Fast as horses, I thought. I nearly ducked

but we found ourselves
enveloped in the muffled womb of nothing
special. Days passed.

The war smelled the same
as the not-war: lilac, musk and mold, the air
wet as a dry tongue. Citizens

still went to market,
held emerald mangoes in their hands,
predicted timelines for ripeness.

One morning when my feet jockeyed my husband's
for warmth in bed
and the upstairs neighbor made the ceiling rattle,

I wondered: had that been the war?
The cherubim on commercials
were flushed and well-fed as before.

Maybe when we slept, the war swept
our hair away like a surgeon's hand.
By night, we learned the death toll,

saw their chiseled faces onscreen,
were never told, beyond *The War*,
what took them. We imagined

they tipped over in a field
like cows engulfed in a gentle, toxic cloud.
Now we watch the fog retract

from the land like a tsunami of smoke
backing down. Now our faces in the windows
stare back at us, our furrowed brows

assuming the V-shaped rendition of birds
a child draws above her bright landscape.
Somewhere mothers are weeping.

Outside, the pointy pines salute a cloud.
The books in our cases are rows of rectangular skylines
still intact. We cannot hear

the weeping. We think
the war has passed, although we admit
we have no proof.

The Best House on the Block

It'll have cathedral ceilings, a view
      no local can afford.
Hammer at rest, one builder shouts
      I wanna leave, I wanna
fucking leave. His marriage? This town?
      Its doors have been closing for
decades. The biggest business
      is fixing bodies. The hospital scoped
my insides five times to find growths
      benign, or babies blessed in goo.
Outside the halfway house
      a woman smokes and stares
toward the town's touristy center
      like a wind will blow her an answer
to some question she's lost
      the energy to ask. Attract the middle class,
says the governor. Visit the grave
      of Robert Frost, says a brochure off the side
of a byway that lets travelers circumvent
      the zip code in which he rests.
Three times a year, an Aussie stands
      among the Unitarian Universalists
and says: *The land does not understand you.*
      Nobody's bothered to talk to it
since the Wabanaki. The east coast urbanite
      newspaper says we're full of opioids.
Older than the Rockies, the mountains beg
      to differ. Like gods
on our landscape of dollar stores
      and dangling shutters, they say *Yes,*
you'll die. But we've seen it
      a thousand times before and you
have nothing to fear. Inside the skeleton,
      hammering resumes. Go ahead,
crew: Build your stellar view.

For One Shutter-Click We Loved Ourselves

Arial view of artichokes
unearthly in their leathery blooms, saying pay
attention, You, to the ordinary awe.

Then scarves half-masking faces,
exhales white as chalk, saying
we are here in sub-zero and alive

and hoping you'll love us, or
documenting that for one shutter click
we loved ourselves

as much as artichokes. I can't tell.
Everything here means more than it is:
an ex-vegan's dinner and a neighbor's

anger and a Big Person's bigger
prize and someone's dead horse.
Beaches are banners over lives landlocked—

Michiganians longing for crab.
The telephone told us to reach out
and touch someone. I reach out. The screen

is slick as a magazine, the artichokes'
reptilian spikes flat as glass. I'll send
across the ether what I want to clutch

eternal: my footy-PJ-ed kids
holding each other in sleep, hairlines
sweaty, fat cheeks filled with dew,

selves not yet performed
for anyone. Catch them, catch them
before they scroll into the night sky

between the billions of stars
so mammoth and bright they send us light
years after they're dead.

Beatitude for the Internet Age

Then one day the lure to snag a crown
dissolved. It happened as my kid and I drew hair
in outer space. Our heads went wild
beneath our bubble helmets, tangles reaching
seaweed-like toward stars. Back on Earth
I watched a peony unfurl and blinked,
ate a slice of awe and didn't think
to recreate its perfect pastry for a prize.
I stopped believing screens, although they throbbed
electric blue, shrunk to the size of keys
that slipped into our ears, whispering *you matter
only if more people say you do*. I broke
like a curse the word *brand*, found half a robin's egg
and didn't wonder where was the other half
so I could logo it for love or praise—
I stopped confusing the two. I showed up hungry
at a church and asked. The stained glass saints
said we've all been where you are now
without the URLs. We wore fewer hairshirts
than you think. Get low, not to repent but to press
your ear to the earth. Listen for the pulse
beneath the billions of you pacing. Hear it?
Soft, subtle—same word you cry for mercy.
Enough enough. But not this time
a begging. *Enough enough*—a blessing.

Domesticity in the Era of Doom

We circle the turned-off radio,
wager whether to let it speak.
Each day, a new announcement:
The Minister of Love is a car salesman
who's presently holding a grudge
against Maine. The Secretary of
Citizenship spits at kids who step
on her lawn. The Agent of Abundance
orders all national gardens
on lockdown, writes an edict
to strangle each fruit-bearing tree.
My love and I are trying to hold
our house together, light candles
before dinner, but a fire killed thirty
artists in Ann Arbor. The lifestyle experts
pretend everything's normal. *Chug water*
is what they tell us, and *Don't do drugs,*
or *Do. Take this pill* and *this one*
but *not in combination.* We scrub
the driveway, shovel the toilet,
and the radio says a dozen state-issued bullets
split a body that held no weapon.
We hold our broom-handles,
look up. The sky has gone
from blue to brick. Should we pray
for the right clouds
or acceptance
of the clouds as they are?

Hurricane Coming

Eyes on a palm-sized screen, I read aloud
the dozen ways doom could knock, fail to see
her eyes water. Her cheeks bulge rubescent
over her cereal bowl. *Why would God
rip off a roof?* I bite inside me the truth
that roofs get wrecked every minute.
*God wouldn't. Not ours. Want more? Yes, ours
is not to reason why. God loves.* But why
do reaches for meaning read like the worst
choose-your-own-adventures, every ending
falling mid-sentence into mud?

The hurricane's a half-day late. We flick
a button to another world, eat popcorn,
watch good and bad push with almost
equal force. Swirls of smoke inhale the life
from knocked-out boys, but the steel sky
is so painted it doesn't quicken her pulse.

Just then, a crack. No wind. The hulkish arm
of an oak falls a hundred feet, lands smack
where ghosts of us munch summer salad.
The table is a pile of glass. The chairs
are now unholy Ls, half-flattened, filled
with limbs and leaves.
                What story will she carry
into her next year? Every tree is a weapon
regardless of weather? She knows by credits' roll
the hero will stand, battered only enough
to be bettered, faint scratch on his chin.
How can I tell her the other endings
are also true? The house is sometimes hollowed,
the angel appears too late, the trapdoor opens
to a field of light too bright for you to see.

Outdoor Church

Our litany of the dead barely lifts
above the engine revs. Is it rage
or rejoicing, the Ford's bass beat?
Prayer in masks means no one can see
my lips unmoving to the creed.
Beneath our feet, the bodies of those
that began with R: Robertson. Rudd.
How did they rage against the machine?
They missed not just this plague
but the last one. Faith is dead
without works, says the priest, like one
in five hundred. The hymn has us
singing about higher ground
while we stand in a town built on sand.
In another two degrees, this all goes under.
You can tell from the bumpers
which trucks wish to war with women
cradling big decisions in their centers,
like the body's first flicker is not
what it is—a door the soul can swing through
saloon-style before tethering itself
in place, the way my mortgage locks me
to this state. *God's Country*, reads a flag
on faded orange shingles. *Don't drive
like hell through it.* Last night's tornado
brought two houses a taste of the end times.
A Category Five is called the finger
of God, but no one's sure which one:
index or middle. We're always in end times.
These ones are just worse because
we're still being sold to. When you buy
a big item like a dishwasher,
they congratulate you. When you die
on a cross to break open the world,
untie every cry from any country,
nobody but God is with you.

[IV]

AMEN

Beyond Chitchat

*Sure, you can use lasers or radiation, but the simplest way
to entangle two particles is to just let them interact.*
— "Quantum Entanglement Explained," YouTube

Can we begin   with matters other than weather?
Tell me the weight   of your dreams

last night as you brought   them into the shower
When your mind   filled out the face

of the masked DMV worker   was she more beautiful
than your late mother?   What about the imperfect globe

of your homegrown tomato   Can it cure hunger?
That's the trouble   Our gestures are so small

they might as well sit   on a trainset of this planet
So we boil down   to how we feel about the day's

peak temperature   We thought the atom
was the smallest thing   then found a dance

of smaller things inside it   If two electrons talk
long enough   you can send one to the edge of space

and keep the other in your pocket   What you do to one
reaches the other   Please explain why

we think we're not the same   Einstein called it *spooky*
didn't understand   that two are sometimes one

despite light years between them   What relief to know
we're not alone so long   as we've once been together

Ovulating in Church

Desire starts just above the eight-inch spikes
affixing his feet to the cross.

His calves are taut as a sprinter's
or those of an old boyfriend in World Religions

who, like me, traded kidhood faith
for oaks and a void of sky.

I've spent all day
in silent prayer, so I'm quick

to catch my mind before it sends
my body toward the rafters, crawling

over crucified Christ's chiseled—
literally chiseled—muscle.

Cut it out, he told his students
of their eyes. I skip the raggedy sarong,

let my eye lay on four ribs and then
below, his gaunt gut, hollowed.

It's a bowl of *ow*, or how, as any
postpartum woman knows,

agony and ecstasy demand our all.
This is what you get, Church, for making God

my size. This is what you get, God,
for making yourself so hard to find.

Minutes later, a priest splits apart the moon-
shaped cracker, and by God

I'll take you into myself
one way or another.

Eve

You think I wanted to burn it all down—that's why I bit.

You forget what it feels like to wear the clothing of a breeze
and not believe your body's been made for that twin display
of hide and peek.

Consider this: I never thrashed against the isolation of a single room,
not even your first, a womb.

I knew one thing. I bit to know two. What is goodness
without its contrast? I had no clue
                                        the world would split
like two sides of a coin, never seeing each other.

Need crept over me like a hooded robe, as it did him.
Then cold, and hunger,

and now none of us knows how to be human without it.

We can't go back. We can only hold each other, let love
strip off the clothing of the self—or what we believe

is the self—
                and tread toward an inner garden we were given
from the start. Please know:

It wasn't always sunny in the garden. It's only that the rain
felt just as right.

Agnostic Visits the Nature Conservatory

The book of Chrysalides
dangles by a pushpin poked
through its half-formed wings.
It hangs, not from an oak,
but from a sterile, coded shelf
encased in perfect weather
to coax the coddled seed of itself.

The book of the Century Plant
never blooms but once in its dry stock
of sand-words and leaf-spikes.
Its bite is bigger than the up-stuck
fingers it calls petals: spite
in the arid sky, Moses stuttering
old names in vain.

But the book of Bonsai, feathering
green on its brown spine, feigns
a hundred decades for its simple three.
Here's your psalm. Stand beside
it, be the giant you'll never be,
the branching of your lungs' bronchi
vast as an inverted tree.

Agnostic Says Morning Prayer

We glory be to your Father, your Son,
and the mistiest of you, lilting
between leaf-edges like the fog
smoking the hills this church
is wedged between.
                      Trinity,
you're a strange family
of one body and no women.

Outside, the school buses screech
to stop, putter waiting, and we say
as it was in the beginning.
This is why I want you back,
want what some call
your second coming: for revision,
every writer's love-hate obsession.
*Kingdom, father, eternal
redemption*—I want you
to rewrite the language of heaven.

And what would I have you say?
Make it about fog, maybe.
Call God a mountain. A mother.
I don't know, Second Jesus,
surprise me. Melt the stained glass
in all these windows as we leap out,
breathe pine, are caught
by angels or very strong women.

Packing for a Silent Prayer Retreat

We need less than we think.

Still, I count ten books, stuff
a hundred songs
into a blipping rectangular glow,

bring thirty circles
of paint and a brush
and paper I won't touch.

I bring fear I can't
keep quiet for
eight whole days,

the belief that the bowl
between my ears
will chastise itself

into oblivion
without distraction to fill it.

They call the rooms *cells*.
The knobs are without locks.
I turn mine:

a bed, a desk, a chair,
and I revisit
what my infant self

most likely sensed
at first breath and bath
of light:

The world is plenty full.

Then we draw maps
to treasure that will never
suffice. I lie down

on the twin mattress
and cry it out—
what mothers say

of babes when they can't
be held. Behold,

the God of all things
is so big
we cannot find her.

News Fast (at a Monastery on the Hudson)

What headlines can we write
of the butterfly?

        That its black velvet
invades blossoms in a land colonized
by air?

      Or of the pines? That
their impossible tallness waves
for lower taxes?

        There is no talk
of nuclear disarmament
in the meadow.

        Everything here
wants no more than it is

except a cargo ship, long as a landing strip
sliding against the river.

        It carries minds
which carry, I surmise, the stream
of this week's headlines.

        Let me guess.
Countries poking sticks in sand,
children in adult
trousers ordering other children
dead, and a glacier

      going
faster than experts' worst dreams.
Every morning I offer the sky
a briefing on this:

        peonies balled
so tightly they look like miniature planets
in pink and white.

We've made TVs that depict
wars clearer than our naked eyes can see
and yet I've never glimpsed
a bud like this,

           so close-fisted
it looks like it could never open
into a softer world.

Canticle of the Ordinary

My daughter picks purple
wildflowers in the borderland
between our yard
          and the neighbor's.
I think of property rights.
She thinks:
      Here, mama.

I pinch the hair-fine stems
to trim them,
      slip them
through the neck
of a two-inch vase.

She won't once
think they'll brown in three days
or in an hour
      blow to the ground.

The world is filled with eight
billion souls
      and none I know
has seen the face of God.

Her run toward
the next wonder—dandelion,
gutter—
      is still living scripture.

Be delighted
in five-petaled stars.
      Let them be
for once not prophets of death
or hope,
      but canticles
of the ordinary, which seems
to be the most holy
      we have.

After a Silent Retreat

How quickly I lose my love
of all things. I nearly flick an ant
off the cliff of an armchair.

But remember, Self,
the week you spent
enveloped in psalms

intoned by monks?
By Wednesday you beheld

a three-balled body
creeping around
the onionskin of your book,

its six teensy toothpick-
legs bent into all manner of
delicate angles?

Your chest became
a doorway
to a spacious unmarked

heaven. You loved the ant.
The kingdom
said Christ,

is at hand, meaning
not ticking above

in a timebomb of gold-
paved streets but
tapping antenna

along the heartline
of your imperfect palm.

ACKNOWLEDGMENTS

A book is a group project, and that's no more apparent than when it's slated for publication. I'm incredibly grateful to the team at Monkfish, including Paul Cohen and Anne McGrath for saying yes, Tanya Murray for her long phone calls and thoughtful editing, and Colin Rolfe for his patient cover-designing. Thank you for championing literary and spiritual work!

Huge thanks to my former poetry professors, David Baker, Kathy Fagan, Stephen Kuusisto, Andrew Hudgins, Fleda Brown, and Jeanne Murray Walker. There are too many Buckeyes to name, but I'm so grateful to the (mid-aughts) MFA community at Ohio State, where some of these poems started. Thank you to poetry pals Maria Williams, Michelle Wiegers, Natalie Shapero and James Crews for offering support, as well as my agent, Anna Knutson Geller. Nancy Reddy's Blue Stoop workshop helped me turn ten-plus years of poems into a book. Thank you, Nancy and the workshop members, for our quarantining community! Thanks to Ellen Bass for an excellent lecture series. And thank you to my employer, Rowan University, for supporting my creative efforts with course releases and continued study.

Many thanks to the editors of the following publications, in which versions of these poems first appeared:

Alaska Quarterly Review: "Skipping Stones"
Barrow Street: "Things I Heard after My Baby Was Born," "The Best House on the Block"
The Briar Cliff Review: "Eve"
Chattahoochee Review: "Sperm"
Cimarron Review: "Bed Rest," "Free Bible in Your Own Language"
The Cincinnati Review: "My Family and I Disagree about Politics"
Crab Orchard Review: "Jesus Might Have Walked on Ice, Scientists Say"
Diagram: "My Form of Yelling"
EcoTheo Collective: "Loving Thy Right-Wing Neighbor"
Failbetter: "Ovulating in Church"
The Florida Review: "Forecast in the Thirty-First Week"
Image: "Psalm for Doctor Normal"

Literary Mama: "Pumping Milk," "The Messiah Could Have Gotten Listeria," & "The World Moves Too Fast"

Mid-Atlantic Review: "Bear Leads Police in Wild Chase"

Monday Coffee and Other Stories of Mothering Children with Special Needs: "Your Eyes, My Daughter, Are Genius Caliber"

The North American Review: "Only a Sliver of Love Runs Hot"

The Path to Kindness: Poems of Connection & Joy: "Your Heartbeat"

Pleiades: "The War We Barely Knew"

Rogue Agent: "Before Writing Back to a Friend Whose Mother Is Dying"

Smartish Pace: "Empire in Your Gut"; *Shenandoah*: "Father Jim Shows Me Twelve Jesuses"

South Carolina Review: "To the Parent Who Says Her Child Isn't in the Natural Order of Things"

Southern Poetry Review: "Rush Hour Commute, Good Friday"

The Southern Review: "Ode to Seven"

The Sun: "Two Weeks after a Silent Retreat"

Unsplendid: "Agnostic Visits the Nature Conservatory"

Wayfarer: "Upon Learning that My Daughter Can Swallow Her Own Spit"

Wordgathering: A Journal of Disability Poetry and Literature: "To the Comic Who Says Her Critic Is Missing a Chromosome" & "Christian Ladies Talk Infertility"

And lastly, my family. I love you. P & F: I'm blessed to be your mom. J+: I am so freaking lucky to have you as my partner. You're the best. A-round.

HEATHER LANIER is the author of the memoir *Raising a Rare Girl* (Penguin 2020), a *New York Times Book Review* Editors' Choice, as well as two award-winning poetry chapbooks. Her work has appeared in *The Atlantic*, *TIME*, *McSweeney's*, *The Sun*, *Longreads*, *The Southern Review*, and elsewhere. She works as an Assistant Professor of creative writing at Rowan University, and her TED Talk, "'Good' and 'Bad' Are Incomplete Stories We Tell Ourselves," has been viewed three million times. You can find her at heatherlanierwriter.com.

Printed in the USA
CPSIA information can be obtained
at www.ICGtesting.com
JSHW082224140824
68134JS00015B/716